Remembering Softly

Remembering Softly

a life in poems

by

Catherine Lawton

CLADACH
Publishing

An AGATES Book of Poetry

Published by Cladach Publishing
Greeley, Colorado 80633
www.cladach.com

Interior art by Isabelle Lawton and Breanna Slike
Cover art: iStock/HolySource

The following poems were first published in print periodicals: "I Have a Friend" in *Junior Joys;* "Window Washer," "Wings of the Spirit," "Footprints in the Snow," "Autumn" and "Blue Asters" in *Living Streams;* "She Prays" in *Prayer Works;* "Antidote" in *Herald of Holiness.*

Library of Congress Control Number: 2016913710
ISBN-13: 9780989101455

Second Printing

Printed in the United States of America

"With eyes wide open to the mercies of God..."
Romans 12:1 (PHILLIPS)

Contents

Introduction

Those of us who enjoy poetry and who compose poetry do so because, for us, nothing quite distills the feelings of a moment as does a piece of rhyming or free verse with its sense, sound, and form.

A poem comes from someplace in the heart. And as it is read, it reveals something about the heart. Like music, it may employ major or minor tones. I hope at least one of the poems in this volume, selected expressions from each stage of my life, will touch a chord for the reader—perhaps in a major key of delight or consolation; perhaps with minor overtones of grief or longing. May you find something here to illumine your path and lighten your soul at whatever place of life you find yourself.

From my wanderings in—and wondering about—nature; from opening more and more to the Divine; from faith, family, and friends; out of noisy living and quiet places; out of whelming emotions, questionings and questing ... come poems to help cope, to make sense of it all, to ennoble earthly life.

In crisis has come hope; in fear has come faith; in fragility has come strength; in joy has come affirmation; in loss has come bounteous grace.

I want to remember it all, but softly.

C. Lawton
September 1, 2016

POEMS FROM ADULT YEARS

in Reverse Chronology

with art by Isabelle Lawton

A Word About These Poems

"Which do you like most? The mountains or the ocean?" My sister and I would ask each other.

I could never decide. In California for much of my life, I didn't have to choose. We had both within close distance. I could look up and see the steadfastness of the Sierras or the Coastal Range with their redwoods, pines, deer, bears, racoons, waterfalls and trout streams that fed the valleys. I could often feel the ocean breezes and smell the salt air from tides so full of power yet knowing their limits, from waves that lapped like earth's heartbeat.

The metaphors we claim as our own come to us from our surroundings like a fawn stepping out of the forest or beach glass glistening in the sand.

"Which season do you like best?" was another question my sister and I would discuss. Winter offered Christmas. Summer offered school-less, barefoot days, swimming and camping. Spring meant orchards in bloom, Easter, newness.

When I returned with my husband in midlife to my native state of Colorado, I found that daily life was even more determined by the seasons here, especially winter and summer. I found that Spring near the Rockies is a matter of winter and summer fighting it out until summer wins a precarious victory.

But fall remains my favorite season, a time of the year that most inspires me to write poems. As I prepare this collection, I find myself in the Autumn of my life. Christmas doesn't bring quite the same delight and anticipation except as our grown children and our six grandchildren share the celebrations with my husband and me. Summer I love in this high country, where wildflowers bloom from spring to early fall, the scent of summer rains on prairie grasses imparts indescribable sweetness, and sunsets paint glorious colors across the wide sky.

But fall ... During this season of life colors have muted a little, most storms have settled, and anticipation of change keeps one mindful that each era of life comes—and then passes. We must gather the harvest, the fruit, the beauty—as I do from my garden—and preserve it, distill it, package it to sustain us in the winter and to share with others.

When we lived near the Pacific Coast of Northern California, we enjoyed hunting for agates at the beach any time of year. Sometimes as a wave receded, we'd see the semi-precious stones tumbling in the gravelly sand. This process had polished them to translucence, often revealing mossy patterns inside, each unique and formed by the accumulated years. Other types of agates are found in the mountains and on the plains. Each of these gems uniquely encapsulates the effects of pressures and changes in the formation of our earth home. Yet, looking deep within each agate elicits a certainty that these natural processes were guided by a beautiful, loving, almighty Creator.

I think poems are like agates.

This week I had a conversation with my sister, who has also written verse. "Where does a poem come from?" we wondered aloud. Sometimes it seems to rise up from some secret place deep within. Other times a poem—or the inspiration for one—seems to come from without. Our grandfather used to say with a twinkle in his eye that he wrote poetry when the "muse sat on his shoulder." To me it seems as if help comes surely, perhaps from a literary angel. In his poem, "*The Country of* Déjà Vu," Wendell Berry asserts that his poems "came through the air, I wrote them down, and sent them on" like migrating birds stopping at his feeder. Perhaps that is as good an explanation as any.

I still marvel at an experience I had in my young adult years. At home with two toddlers, my husband busy with his career, I was emotionally bound up by griefs and losses, especially the death of my mother. I hadn't written a poem for a long time. One evening I went by myself to a poetry reading at a religious retreat center near our home. I knew no one there. The woman poet read with warmth from verses full of life and light and love. I didn't go expecting this to happen; but, somehow, soaking in the spoken rhyme, rhythm, and sense, awakened the gift in me. For months after that evening, poems began freely coming to mind. The opening of this fountain provided one part of the healing the Lord began working in and through me, which continues today.

Admittedly, I am not a disciplined poet. I can compose meter and rhyme on demand; but mostly I wait for that elusive and mysterious inspiration. The important thing is to capture on paper the phrases, images, and insights as they come; to sit with them, savor them, polish them like agates; and if they pass the test of holding together and ringing true, to share them.

I won't limit each poem's meaning by trying to explain the emotions and experiences that, for me, are encapsulated in each one. As I send them out, they are free to take on new meanings as each reader looks into them. Perhaps for you a poem will speak to a quandary, a sorrow, or a joy you are experiencing at this season of your life. That is the beauty of sharing a gift of poetry.

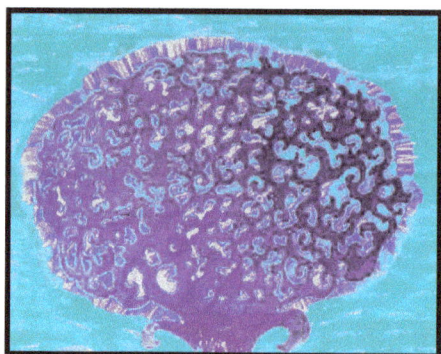

In the Cleft of a Cold White Rock

As in the close space
between dawn and dusk
of a January day when
hoar-frosted trees
have their feet in snow
and their branches
raised against a white,
weighty sky, a crevice
of blue breaks and
frosted arms sparkle;
I find myself pressed
between granite slabs,
as it were, longing for
warm feet, for light to
lift and reassure.
God put Moses in a
cleft of the rock and
showed him His back.
I desire also His face.
Then, like a split of
brilliance in the clouds,
His hand lifts and I see
His trailing glory and
that He has been here
all along. And I know
without seeing that
He is smiling.

January, 2016

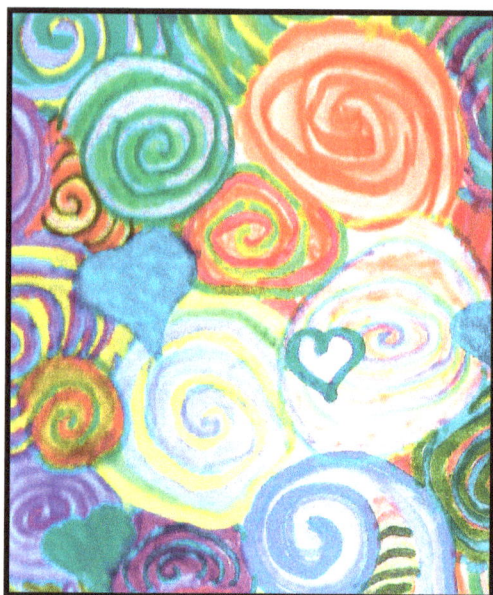

Weights of Glory

Flying over mountains
from familiar-coast visit,
with more weight—not
from laden carry-on
or well-fed tummy
but re-filled heart
and mind, full of
kindred connections
and added memories,
with news and views,
insights, sensations
which now I hold and
carry back—or
they hold, enfold me,
these glorious weights,
entwining and lifting,
this knowingness
of love.

July, 2015

Earth and Heaven

As wind in the forest bends the trees
with sounds of whooshing and unearthly creaks,
in Sunday sanctuary where footfalls creak wood,
both moved and moving, both chosen and choosing;
with thoughts of earth and songs of Heaven,
with longings and doubts, with tears and petitions;
the creaking of dry souls as elements are passed—
whispers like sweet breezes flow down the pew,
saying, "This is His body broken for you."

June, 2015

Snow On Good Friday

We grieve when snow falls
on Good Friday eve.
What about the greening,
the beginnings of spring? when
like manna fallen from Heaven—
"My body broken for you" into
flakes and crumbs—
soft, pure-white flesh
spread upon all that lies
both dormant and sprouting,
at morn reflects the rising sun;
except in rockiest places,
saturates fallow and seeded,
both broken and wasted ground.

April, 2015

God's Anvil

I've known some prophets
burning with a message
burdened with desire
longing to witness
renting of heaven
repenting of sin
Acts for today
as the church
re-awakens
to purity
power
love.

July, 2015

A Choice

With God's help
I move beyond
discouragement
and uncertainty.
By God's grace
I choose
not to let my
feelings and failures
undo or hinder
all the good that
God has done
and desires to do
for us and in us
and through us.
The joy of the Lord
is my strength.

2015

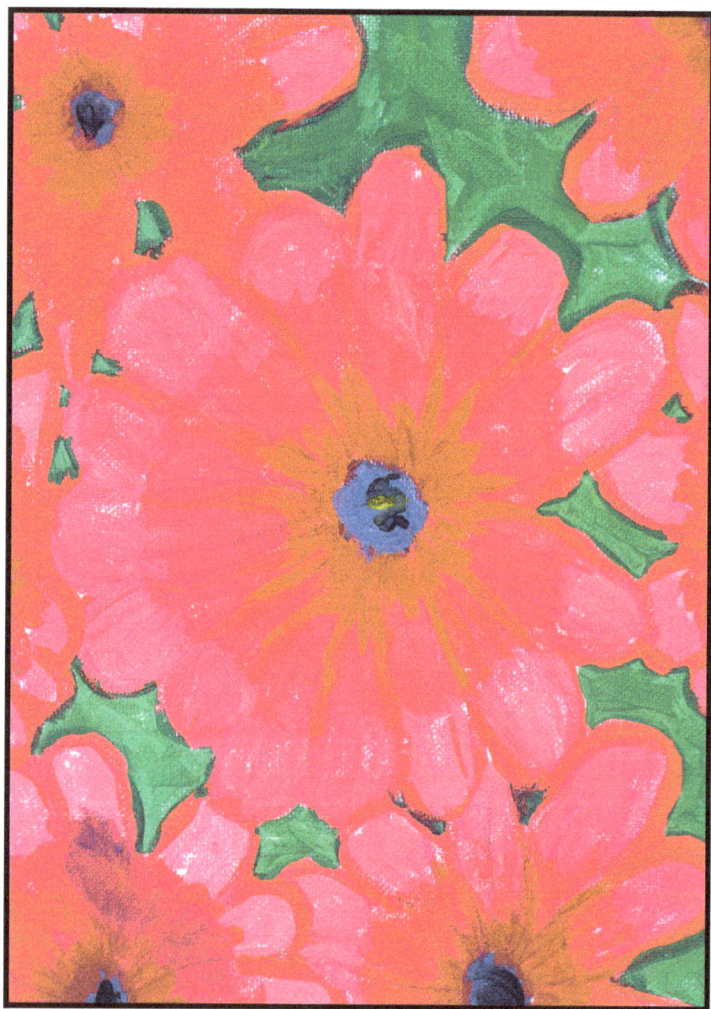

Glory

Could this be true?—
  I've heard the story
that believing souls
  are filled with glory.

Glory?!—and holy Love,
  that powerful sway
that gives, creates—
  always . . . always.

I'm not always anything—
  now hearing, now not;
with clay feet bound,
  with failure wrought.

But Love's radiant force
  enlightens, surrounds,
pursues and woos
  as Heaven's hound.

'Twill find a way
  with water and fire
to seep, to burn
  into stony mire;

On heart of flesh
  to write the story
of life transforming
  from glory to glory.

March, 2015

Gladwin—

So I'll call you—cheerful,
friend, and so much more.
Powerful, flaming, bright,
from heights I can't explore.

But a voice that cries out, "Stop!"
when I drive too close to danger;
A wake-up knock at dawning day,
when this traveler mustn't linger.

A young man—fair, attentive—
with perception, help, and humor
came and left, unseen by others—
left me lifted, filled with wonder.

A rustling wind in grove of trees
that bid me pause to look and hear
soft, silvery songs of tiny birds
on trunk and branch appear.

As I lay on bed of sickness,
weak and fading, I could feel
someone stood unseen beside me,
touched the places Christ would heal.

Both you and I have God to thank—
He's *our* Creator and *my* Father—
the One you gaze upon and serve;
Who helps me see, attune, and follow.

He thought to send His guardians down
to be with us until we're home,
to deliver His messages and protect;
to help us know we're not alone.

March, 2015

A Man With a Sword

(for Larry)

He's not a soldier—not in that sense,
  or a pirate who steals and plunders,
  or a knight who's storming castles.
He's a man, a man with a sword.

Who as a child was taught to sheath it;
  in his youth, he learned to wield it;
  in his prime, was never without it.
In old age, it gives him courage.

He has notches to prove his prowess,
  the stance of ready self-knowledge,
  the strength of hardy self-control,
and a blade as sharp as love.

A soldier who carries scars of glory,
  a pirate with swashbuckling stories,
  a knight guarding good and right;
he's a man, a man with a sword.

September, 2014

Consolation

Sweet blue flowers
  gracing spring
  don't last.
Tough yellow blooms
  of late summer
  smile on
  through moons
  of waning days
  and cheer us
  into fall.

August, 2014

In My Heart an Altar

While I stand here before the Lord
   or sit and meditate,
My heart still at an altar bows;
   and that I contemplate.

An altar by my parents stood,
   with me a babe in arms,
As prayers were said and ordinance read
   with oil to dedicate.

An altar called and I stepped forth.
   conviction in my heart;
And there I knew the Father made
   His child regenerate.

At altarside my husband joined
   his hand and heart with mine;
And as we walk this path in sync,
   the Altar consecrates.

Together we have sought and learned
   and folded children in;
The family altar kept us close,
   a bond to celebrate.

And when I stand or sit or kneel,
   the elements receive—
My heart an altar—death and life
   still bid me to partake.

2014

Longing For Home

The place of warmth,
comfort, peace, joy,
fellowship, laughter,
acceptance, knowing,
family, food, flowers,
music, grace, forgiveness.

I try to make the place
I find myself in feel like Home,
comfortable and expressive,
to please and fit, rejuvenate.

Are heart rest and satisfaction
ever complete without the people
we love there as well?—
at least knowing they're safe
in harbor, warm and fed.

Growing up, home was where my
parents were, and my sister.
Sometimes together we left, returned,
enjoyed, longed for ... home. We didn't
provide home for each other but did
provide assurance and a shared hope
that there was home somewhere.

Together we sang,
"I've Got a Mansion
Just Over the Hilltop,"
"Surely Goodness and Mercy
Shall Follow Me ...
And I Shall Dwell in the
House of the Lord Forever."

February, 2013

Friends

We don't just love
our friends because
they're worthy. No,
we love them for
times spent together,
memories made; the
times we've glimpsed
their hearts and felt
that they've seen ours,
and recognized
our foibles too—
and still we're
friends.

December, 2013

Sitting In the Grass
On an Autumn Day

I sit with my dog on damp, green grass
  in dappled shade of apple trees
    gilded by slanting sun.

I comb my fingers through puppy fur
  to music of bees that seek the last
    drops from shrivelling blooms.

The teasing, teethy breezes blow down
  snowy peaks, across cornfields,
    then tousle my silver-streaked hair.

I'd hold this moment; but I can't.
  It holds me, though, and carries me
    to the next and the next and ...

October, 2011

Deborah

A fierce and beautiful woman
  who inspired courage in men;
Sought out for wisdom and judgment;
  trusted to lead and to win.

A woman who listened and let God
  beat on the drum of her heart;
Marching to danger with faith,
  speaking God's words from the start.

Not full of self—neither loathing,
  nor doubt nor concern—but aligned.
Giving and going and serving
  in front of, beside, and behind.

Sure in times of uncertainty,
  faithful when others despair;
Lifting the flagging to valor,
  singing the victory aire.

October, 2010

After Our Family Reunion

In a corner of a window well a ray of sun
warms a toad who swells and puffs
in and out, in and out, in and out.

He listens to the ringing silence now
and sees Grandma look at him and
smile and sigh, smile and sigh, smile and sigh.

The house exhales with sleepy joy
remembering footsteps, laughter, voices
play and sing, play and sing, play and sing.

The old eyes, the child eyes, the telling eyes,
the asking eyes above smiles of wonder—
open, close doors, open, close, open, close.

He waits for more of the vibrations that
stirred the house to warmth and sound,
up and down, in and out, round about.

One by one the motors all roll away.
But memories and sensations linger
of sharing and holding and releasing you.

July, 2010

God's Inexplicable Work
A Prayer

I feel I'm in a process
of getting in touch with
something You are doing
    INSIDE OF ME,
as I take moments
to be still.
I come close, skirt the edges,
receive glimpses...
    LORD,
help me see, acknowledge,
receive, open my heart;
please keep doing your
merciful, inexplicable
    WORK—
whether I see fully or not.

March, 2010

Living Wounds

Christ's wounds—
holes, gaps, gashes?—
remain, continue there,
healed; no pain or festering.
But they remain
places on the body
of the God-Man,
remembering.
A mystery!
There,
in the wounded place
we are part of Christ.
The nails are gone,
the sword withdrawn,
the thorns pulled out.
But these wounds live,
efficacious.
When His followers also
stand gashed and riddled,
touching our wounds to His;
bearing scars from
our own sins and
those of others
but festering no more,
together we form
places of healing
in the body of Christ.

2009

Autumn Walk
Along the Poudre River

I go down by the river in autumn breeze
  that quakes gold leaves on craggy trees
  and skitters dry ones at my feet.

The chill breeze hints of snowy peaks,
  lifts cricket songs, soars hawks on high,
    sails wispy clouds across clear-blue sky.

I see Kingfisher, Yellow-legs, bright Magpie;
  hear squirrels chatter, Red-tails scream,
  and splashing fish in sparkling stream.

God said that all He made was good;
  and surely all these things are good;
  and everything He does is good.

My senses and soul exult in our God—
  who made seasons of change and decay
  to display His unchanging glory.

October, 2009

Rhymes for Grandchildren
born 2003-2014

God Bless the Baby

Upon learning our first grandchild was on the way and seeing the parents leading in worship (later I was meditating on these things and out came a rhyme in the form of a chanted prayer).

Oh, Sweet Baby,
Little baby Lawton.
Baby, do you hear it?
Hear your daddy praying?
Baby, do you hear them?
Blessed little baby.

God bless Hannah;
Bless her little baby.
Let it hear the singing,
Hear her heart's devotion,
Make the Maker real,
Present every moment.

God bless David;
Bless his little baby.
Let it hear the praying,
Hear the strong assurance,
Feel the Father's nearness,
There for His baby.

Oh, Sweet Baby,
Little baby Lawton,
Baby, do you hear it?
Hear your daddy singing?
Hear your mama praying?
Baby, do you hear them?
God bless the baby.

March, 2003

Isabelle age 4

Isabelle has a room of her own
  with lots of space
where books, toys, and animals roam
  and Kitty plays.

Just go up the stairs,
  turn left and go through,
and you'll be there.
  Wish I was too!

Matthew age 3

Matthew has collected a bunch of little cars,
Matchbox and Hot Wheels. Given a push,
they rev up their engines and go fast and far.

Ask him what kind, and he'll give the answer:
Chrysler, Camaro, Toyota Prius,
Tacoma, Mercedes, and Sport Sedan Lancer.

Breanna age 3

Bright smile
Reaching
Energetic
Adept
Ndearing
Nto
A grandma's heart

Caden age 2

(little rhymes said while rocking him)

Lover boy
Sweetie pie,
Goodness,
What a guy!

Rock-a-bye
Rock-a-bye
Rock-a-bye, boy
Rock-a-bye
Rock-a-bye
Oh, what joy!

Sebastian age 4

"Grandma, I wish
you could stay a
little bit longer."
Your sweet voice
melts my heart,
and I agree:
A few more trips to the sea,
walks in New England leaves;
A few more lunches at LaSalle's
and cones at Canton creamery;
A few more chances to play
Ninja and Lego with Grandpa
and over-the-bed dodgeball;
A few more pretend adventures
with stuffed animals and cars;
A few more picture books
to read on laps and
bedtime stories and
goodnight prayers.
Just a few more...
a little bit longer,
please.

Tiffany age 1

Our number six, Tiffany
is a daughter of Cliff, any
one can see,
and Christina—
which makes her pretty.

Waves On the Cladach

Upon our hearts His words will fall,
   and we'll arise and heed the call.
Cling not to life nor drift in vain;
   set out by faith in Jesus' name.

Upon the shore the waves will break,
   and forth we'll sail, adventures take.
A bon voyage, a welcome home—
   stories to tell. We bid you come.

2004

After Saying Good-bye

Reeling here again on
  smooth but grainy strand,
Lacking grit to lift
  each foot up rocky land.

Turning toward the lure
  in memory's foamy splash,
Tasting salty joys that
  cling from seasons past.

Swelling, surging tides
  now whorl in lonely waves,
Gulfing sense in brine.
  I grope some hold to save.

Dropping empty-handed
  but solid on the shore;
Hearing tides commanded,
  "This far and then no more."

As deep calls to deep,
  I make peace with the depth.
Heading toward the cliffs,
  I take an upward step—

With an ocean in my heart.

2002

If I Hadn't Looked

If I hadn't looked out the window
into the drizzly winter gray,
I wouldn't have seen
the Rufous-sided Towhee
venture from his brambly cover
and flash color
into my ordinary thoughts.

If I hadn't looked out the window,
away from bed making,
I wouldn't have seen
the hawk that dared to
perch on the kid's jungle gym,
larger than life,
contemplating Larkfield rodents.

If I hadn't looked out the window,
just chewing my sandwich,
I wouldn't have seen
the quail parents bravely
march eight downy youngsters
across the street
to sheltering junipers on this side.

If I hadn't looked out the window
with my hands in dish water,
I wouldn't have seen
the curious little owl
hunched in the fruitless mulberry,
waiting silently
within meters of the pane.

Curtains help, keeping out
piercing heat, biting cold, prying eyes;
but windows provide vistas unexpected.
And if I hadn't looked ...

2001

On a Walk In Ferndale

Aggregate sidewalks cracked;
the artful fences gracing thorny
roses, cypress, Redwoods;
curving roads and lanes.

Air thick and moist
with drizzle sent from rolling, rough
waves that cast and pull
nearby on gritty sand.

Green-spiked hills
are catching wisps of fog like lacy
gauze as blanket lifts.
Lawns, not seeded sod,

Thick green carpets
grow tough blades and ferny weeds;
mosses root in soil
black, rich and lumpy.

Houses gingerbread-trimmed
have stood proud a dozen decades,
braving sudden jolts and
countless coats of paint.

People wizened and wrinkled,
give cryptic greetings with so much
left unsaid in ruts
sitting between their words.

No slick answers heard,
no smooth and glassy surfaces—
but weathered and real.

1998

A Walk At Dusk

I took a walk at dusk,
trees silhouetted against
the pink and fading sky,
the hills awash in gold.

Unbidden, I felt Mother close—
in my heart, more than mind,
heard laughter, felt her joy.
Then, as it would be, music—

Majestic, full-piped organ
thrilled the ears of my soul
with strains of "Jesus Shall Reign"
in strings, flutes, and brass.

While heavenly organs play,
tell me, Death, if you can:
Where's your sting? And Grave:
Where is your victory?

January, 1996

Affirmation

(inspired by St. Patrick)

Christ is above me
lifting my vision.
He is below me
upholding my soul.
He is beside me,
encouraging today.
He is before me,
leading the way.
He is behind me,
protecting from the fray.

April, 1991

Evening Light

(during a walk in Larkfield)

Just before twilight,
the sun's gentle good-bye
supplants harsh clarity
with a rosier view.
Golden hues bathe the landscape,
slowly but quickly easing away.
I want to hold this farewell
to a day that will never come again
and remember it all—but softly.

1991

THREE "FIRST" POEMS
FOR DAVID

First Day of School

Big Yellow School Bus,
  why are you in such a rush
to take my little boy away
  to his first school day?

Wake 'im up, "Get out of bed,"
  make sure both his socks are red.
Eggs and toast, butter and honey;
  forty cents milk money.

Hair combed, teeth brushed,
  out the door ready to rush.
Stopping to kiss me the same way
  he's watched his dad do each day.

I'm glad to see him take this step
  with such eagerness and pep.
But, School Bus, as you're drawing near,
  will you overlook one tear?

Where's the tot trailing yellow blankie,
  blue eyes smiling up at me?
He is still my pride and joy,
  Big Little School Boy.

September, 1979

First Home Away

Big college dormitory,
  do you understand the story
of our son who's gone to stay
  down your hall so far away?

Will you give him tender care,
  help him when life deals unfair?
Do you know his special needs?
  Will you see that he succeeds?

Keep him of his manners mindful,
  foster choices that are rightful;
listen late into the night,
  till his headlights come in sight?

You may have a useful function
  at this restless child-man junction.
Our advice has had its say;
  now he has to find his way.

He can call for sympathy;
  bring home friends and laundry.
You'll be there to watch the flight test
  of this fledgling from the home nest.

We'll pay and pray and intercede
  until he's properly degreed.
We'll watch as God unfolds His plan
  for our Big College Man.

September, 1992

First Sent To People Far

Big land so far away,
  do you know who's come your way?
He heard the call and he has gone;
  to become a Francophone.

Do you know that he was sent
  by family and friends to represent
  to you the faith of a higher Son
  who left His home to seek His own?

Will you hear what his French says,
  feel the Touch behind his ways,
  see the Smile behind the fun,
  accept the Gift behind this one?

The years of life he spends in your land
  will return abundantly to his hand.
You and he can help each other
  if you'll respond and say, "My brother."

However many hearts receive
  may he continue to believe
  that God will keep what He's been given;
  and a giving life's the one worth livin'.

We will rejoice in our grown son
  who keeps expanding our horizon.
We'll write and call and always carry
  in our hearts this missionary.

April, 1998

God Plus One
Is a Winning Majority

*(a song written in response
to a challenge)*

God plus one is a winning majority.
God plus one is a winning majority.
If God is for us, who can be against us?
God plus one will win the victory.

The gates of Hell shall not prevail against us,
The gates of Hell shall not prevail against us,
For He is the Lord of Hosts,
Captain of a mighty army,
He's the One who gives the victory.

God plus one is a winning majority.
God plus one is a winning majority.
If God is for us, who can be against us?
God plus one will win the victory.

1987

A River Is Flowing

*(a song inspired by a sermon preached
by an evangelist from Africa)*

There flows now a river
from out of the Throne,
and all who will go there
full cleansing may know.
Your Savior stands ready
to plunge you beneath.
Now rest in His arms—
all your striving can cease.

He'll dip you into the
clear water that flows.
He sees all your sickness;
your heart He well knows.
The dryness, the sadness,
the shame washed away;
your sins all forgotten,
full joy come to stay.

That river will take you—
just yield to its flow;
wherever He leads,
in His power you will go.
There's nothing can stop
the increase of that stream.
It flows with a purpose—
mankind to redeem.

All victory, all healing
all might will be yours,
when out of your heart
Living Water will pour.
Now you can be one with
the Source of that flow.
Praise God for the water!
Our God we can know.

February, 1984

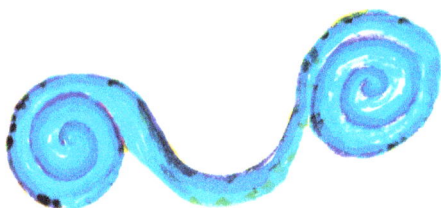

Cleansing, Healing
and Deliverance

(a revival song)

Jesus shed His precious blood
    so I could claim His righteousness.
He has broken down the walls
    of my sin and rebelliousness.

Jesus shed His precious blood
    so that I could claim His peace.
He has taken out my strife
    with His cleansing and release.

Jesus shed His precious blood
    so that I could claim His joy.
He has given me His Life
    and forever I'll rejoice.

1985

Footprints In the Snow

Gently fall—
　holy crystals,
　Son-pure;
　　cleanse this clay.

So white—
　the whitest things
　of earth
　　look gray.

So bright—
　the hidden corners
　of my soul
　　His light displays.

So soft—
　His footsteps can
　impress my heart
　　and show the Way.

1983

He Calms the Storm

Lord, You see me flailing in the storm,
    failing myself and others.
I nearly succumb to the assaulting blast,
    craving oblivion.

Your voice rebukes the inner squall.
    I stop thrashing and fall still.
I cannot stand to look at myself
    but fix my eyes on You.

Please heal the scars. Remake me again,
    more than ever Yours.
With a word, You call into being that
    which didn't exist before.

Your free-flowing, resurging vitality
    infuses raw material.
I rise to move by the wind of Your breath,
    every motion in You.

Amen.

1983

Window Washer

We need to perceive the truth,
yet darkly we peer through the glass.
  Clean me for use,
  free me to serve,
  lift me to reach,
that I may wash windows for You.
  Wrong doctrine obscures;
  gray living besmears;
  raw weather, it blurs
  the pane on this side.
Provide a soft cloth—not abrasive,
the vision to transcend the obstructive,
and courage to rub for perfection—
  searching,
  editing,
  polishing;
till, through one clear corner
  someone sees You.

1981

Antidote

Some things in this world make me mad—
  but I cannot live with hate.
The One whose anger had no sin
  plants His love within.

Some things in this world frighten me—
  but I cannot live in fear.
The One who calmed the thundering storm
  keeps me safe and warm.

Some things in this world are abhorrent to me—
  but I cannot live in disgust.
The One who cast the demons out
  gives a victory shout.

Some things in this world vex my nerves—
  but I cannot live in tension.
The One who took all mankind's stress
  gives vitalizing rest.

1981

God's Husbandman

(for Grandpa G.B.C.)

Thank God for the prophet:
  he cultivates righteousness,
  tills eternal soil,
  plants truth,
  sleeps soundly, no struggles with gray.
He sees black clearly, determinedly
  denounces sin,
  sprays bugs,
  chops weeds,
  calls wayward branches to repentance.
Protecting the pure vigor of his vines,
  he hoes the straight, even rows;
  always sure,
  convinced of right, that
  Light is always white.

Lord, help us receive what's from You,
  and leave the rest, as he
  works to feed us by words
  and example.

July, 1981 (edited 2018)

Beauty

(for Grandma Dorothy C.)

Mirror lights
plastic bottles
labels promise
sensuous appeal
and ageless
beauty.
Yet the
most beautiful
woman I knew
didn't depend on
the sheen, for she shone
with radiance that wasn't
applied
but imparted.

1981

A Friend

Is it chemistry
    or genes
    or symbiosis
    or a lack of halitosis?

Is it clairvoyance
    or enjoyance
    or fate—
    this tete-a-tete?

    No.

It is a gift,
God's love-gift:
a friend.

1980

Wings of Faith

I spun my prayer out of
yearning words,
sighs
and gossamer hopes,
and hung it by a promise
on the strongest branch
I could find.
I gave myself to my prayer.
Rains,
doubts,
cold assailed.
The darkness seemed the only reality.
But I hid within my prayer, and
just as I began to feel lost or forgotten,
it was time.
Faith broke through.
Light dazzled.
I had wings!

February, 1980

Why Me?

Why me, Lord?
What have I done to exact
such treatment—grief and pain?
Sins of commission, neglect, or pride?
The object of divine wrath received,
cruel punishment or heartless testing
that belies promises naively believed?
Why should my days be sacrificed
to folly, weakness, pain?
Why don't you do
something, Lord?

"I've done it all already."

Are those
Your words and is that
You hanging there in pain?
Then why the tender look, as if
it were a joy to die for these ingrates?
The cross did seem a hopeless waste,
and yet those eyes of love attract—
enthrall with mercy, power, and grace,
until I see none other and rejoice
that I, though so unworthy, may be
privileged to share in suffering,
of your life partake.
Why me, Lord?

January, 1980

Blue Asters

By yellowing gherkin vines burdened with fruit,
and moist, black holes yielding carrot roots,
a clump of blue asters have grown up high,
now fading, white-tipped, into autumn sky.

Their dried petals ruffle in wind like the feathers
of bluebirds hovering in defiance of weather,
who, catching crisp hints of frost on the wind,
give in to the breezes and brightly ascend.

I think I would like to go, too, on the wing,
to where I had freedom to dance and sing;
but the bachelor button and I are bound,
I tending the hearth; he feeding the ground.

Then when I have given and finished my share,
I'll rise from the earth to new life in the air.

November, 1979

Leafy Lament

I'm raking leaves and raking leaves,
   scrape, scrape, scraping leaves;
reds and oranges, greens and yellows,
   all the crispy, crunchy fellows
   in soft piles under the big
   Mulberry trees.

Leaves are falling all around me,
   on my head, before, behind me,
making mockery of my raking,
   all my nice green lawn o'ertaking.

It's a leafy, leafy world
   as the trees their glory hurl.
Oh, I need a vacuum sweeper,
   or a giant tree-leaf eater.

November, 1979

She Prays
(for Eloise)

For the family that God gave her,
brothers, sisters, foes and neighbors;
when her heart cries out within her, then
she prays.

When a sweet breeze bathes the soul,
when her cup of joy o'erflows,
receiving faith so free and heartening, glad
she prays.

When no evidence is given,
and the door slams locked to Heaven;
tho' knocking sounds like brash presumption, still
she prays.

Trusted formulations fail,
black and white turn gray and stale,
feeling answer-less, frail, bewildered, on
she prays.

Learning not to give advice
to the God who asks a price.
Through painful crushing and remolding, broken
she prays.

Not content with weak petitions,
seeking miraculous transitions,
trusting Christ, the reigning Victor, bold
she prays.

Love for love will recompense.
Trust ye not in circumstance.
Yes, God hears her and He answers, when
she prays.

November, 1979

It's Fall

It's Fall
  apple-luscious and pie-wonderful,
  chilling bones,
    bringing sweaters,
      misting mornings.
Anticipation fills the air and
  changes stir our hearts,
as leaves—
  crisp and yellow,
  rustle, flutter, skitter,
  carpeting the ground,
where pumpkins,
  orange and plump,
    assembled midst mulch
      and dying vines,
  seem to laugh, when
a squirrel,
  busy, happy,
  scurries, reaping, stashing
    (he knows he'll be prepared).
Like him,
  we gather, store, and celebrate,
  counting blessings, we offer praise,
    heart-felt and wonder-filled,
for provision, for plenty, for family—
  individuals, together,
  laughing, praying, dreaming;
where love brings a harvest of joy
  to share,
  as we watch the colored leaves
  Fall.

1979

Shadows

Murky, oppressive, threatening,
   the darkness sneers at me, accuses,
     attempts to ensnare me;
intent on my destruction, this shadow of death.

Sooty tendrils entwine my heart,
   strangling, corroding, choking.
Must I suffocate without a light to pierce
   this malevolence?
Must I become one with the darkness?
   I will not!

I gasp the name of The One Who is Light.
   The darkness personified backs away
   begrudgingly, but fearing
   the light that gently warms
   like rays of sunshine permeating
   the tangled forest of my heart.

The light is bright.
   I am exposed.
My darkness will show—but no!
The very exposing is a cleansing,
     healing,
     energizing.
I will be one with the Light.

A sweet wind draws a protective shadow,
   soothing, transparent, peaceful,
   intent on my deliverance.
Here I find refuge, here I am free,
hiding in the shadow of His wings.

1978

Release

Lord, free us
from yesterday's
snagging talons
flinging us through
winds that should be fresh,
wringing with beating strokes
of foul resentment,
stinging with poking points
of poisonous suggestions.
Reveal how our reaction
wrenches the claws deeper.
Expose our clutching, clenched
fists; give will to action
   in release.
   We have a choice.
   May your voice
   be all we heed.
Your lifting wing
   is all we need
   to reach the sky.

1978

Autumn

The suntan lost
in teasing of frost.
Leaves swirl everywhere.
Anticipations tinge the air.
Cornstalks point ghostly fingers,
and brittle pumpkin patches linger—
'mid skeletal remains of summer's fare.

With shorter days
the chilly air stays.
No time to laze on hearth,
like bulbs at rest in the earth.
But thanking God, in riches blessed,
we store, like squirrels, the glad harvest.
Without the winter, how comes spring's mirth?

1979

Renewal

"I'm praying you'll have the joy
    of the Lord," you say,
as your eyes reach into mine
    to pull out something hidden.
My heart springs with incredulity
    that you would care, and that
God would meet us there, at the point
    of mutual concern.
For it's happened!
And now I know why wintry despair
    has broken into sudden joy.
A tear wells glistening in the corner
    of your eye,
like the first spring puddle
that speaks of warming and thawing,
    and showers to come.
Is the tear for me?
Or from long-dormant but longed-for
    assurance of Divine quickening?
A tiny drop to spill and flow into
    rivers of awakening.

1978

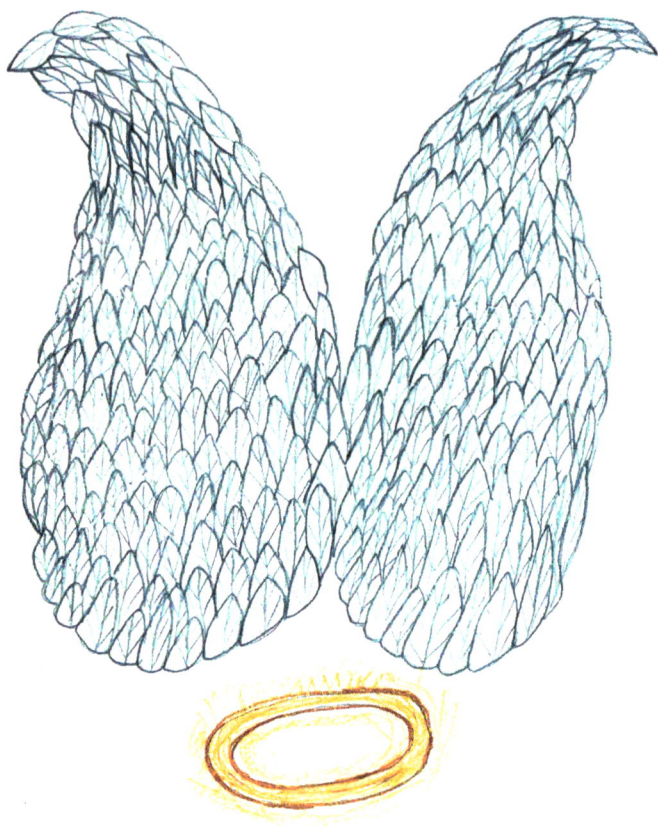

Sleep, Baby

(A lullaby for Christina
at two months)

Sleep, little baby, in your crib so white;
Sleep serenely through the night.

If you awaken and are afraid,
Mommy will hold you and stroke your head.

When Mommy must have her rest too,
Angels stand near to comfort you.

October, 1977

POEMS FROM
CHILDHOOD AND TEEN YEARS

composed under the pen name
Katy Estell

with illustrations by Breanna Slike

A Word About These Poems

One late summer day, at the age of ten, I was riding my bicycle down a street of small houses with no sidewalks in a sleepy valley town of California. My father, mother, sister, and I had just moved to this place surrounded by peach and almond orchards, where Daddy had been called to pastor a church. I would soon start fifth grade in a school where I knew no one except my sister, who was in the grade below me and would have a different recess time. I was missing my friends in my former town, not yet knowing I would form even deeper friendships in this place. Neither did I know that my fifth-grade teacher would inspire me to start writing poems.

That might have been one of the first times I had taken off riding my bike by myself. With sunshine warming my back and wind in my face, whizzing past bungalows, patchy crabgrass lawns, picket fences in various stages of disrepair, here and there a walnut tree, trumpet vine or Oleander bush, I felt a new sense of freedom. In the back of my mind, no doubt, lurked the fact that we had just moved—again. This was about the sixth house I had lived in, and there would be many more. This fed a restless spirit in me and, along with the fact I was "the preacher's daughter" and "the new girl in school," a strong sense of being "different" was heightened by constant reminders that, as Christians, we were "in the world but not of it."

The need to belong resides deep in a person. We belonged to the church, to our denomination, and to the local congregation, some of whom welcomed and treated us like family. We belonged to each other.

As I rode my bike that dusty summer day in pedal pushers, T-shirt, and flip-flops, I was awakening to the awareness that "I" was more than part of my family, part of the church, the school, the community. "I" had to make choices, had to steer my course in one direction or another. At the same time, "I," in ten years, had accumulated a unique set of experiences that made me "me."

When I was four, moves to new places became overwhelmingly scary. Daddy had taken his first pastorate. We had lived in the parsonage only a few days when the house burned down in the middle of the night and we lost everything. After that, my life was shadowed by the memories of escaping through a smoke-filled, flaming living room, siren-blaring fire engines pulling into our front yard, and then later poking through ashes for anything to salvage.

Clearly I remember thinking, as I pedalled my bicycle that day, *What if our house burned down again? What if this time we had time to grab one thing to save from the flames? What would I grab?* I considered the doll that Grandma had given me for Christmas, my new school dress and shoes, my key skates with which I had enjoyed many happy hours skating on the sidewalks in our previous neighborhood. ... I didn't have many personal possessions. But my mind settled on the white leather, zippered Bible Mother and Daddy had given me along with the advice, "Start by reading the red words. Those are Jesus' actual words. ... He will speak to you!"

I made a deeper decision that day as I rode my bike—one of the rare moments of life when we are on the cusp of letting go of the way things have been and stepping into something new—than I realized at the moment. I didn't know why I felt so exultant. It just felt good to say: "I'd get my Bible first!" From then on, I kept it close to my bed at night, within quick reach.

I think the Bible represented for me the One who kept calling us forward into uncertainty and newness, the one thing that was certain and constant, a tangible connection with the intangible but ever-present, all-knowing, almighty One who I somehow knew was there. This Presence was there awakening my heart during the singing and prayers at church; tapping on my shoulder when I was angry, fearful or ashamed; smiling with me when I was absorbed in pure fun with my sister and friends.

Since that day, I have faced many choices to turn to the right or the left. In most instances, I wasn't absolutely sure. I offered myself in surrender to the Lord; I asked for guidance. But the still, small voice must be received by faith. In taking a first step, I didn't ever know where (all) the road would take me. Looking back now, though, I see that, in spite of my fears, weaknesses, and uncertainties—a certain Someone was shepherding me along goodly paths.

In this section, I leave out my maudlin, teenage laments and include poems that are youthful affirmations of faith, love, and joys of life.

Meditation

When the world has turned against me,
   when it seems nobody cares,
Christ is always there to cheer me,
   and He answers all my prayers.

When Satan lays a snare to tempt me,
   and I'm full of doubts and fears,
I just ask the Lord to help me,
   and He gently dries my tears.

I'll never sink with such a Friend!
   In a troubled sea to swim,
I know how to fight the storms—
   just close my eyes and talk to Him.

Day Dreams

I've sailed serenely up the Thames
    and skied down sloping Alps.
I've galloped out across the moors
    and seen the Irish elfs.

I've worn rich gowns and sable furs,
    and expensive French perfumes.
I've gone in golden carriages
    to waltz in crystal rooms.

I've scanned the silent ocean depths
    in search of hidden treasure.
I've taken rides on elephants
    just to fill my pleasure.

I've been a dancing wood nymph,
    a mermaid in the sea.
I've slid down silvery moon beams
    and sung the songs of glee.

I've been a million places
    and seen a million things
By wishing many wishes
    and dreaming many dreams.

A Book

If I'm reading a book,
   it is my whole world.
It's my magic carpet,
   and away I'm swirled—
   off to places unknown.
And I find myself
   living in a strange realm—
   this book off the shelf.

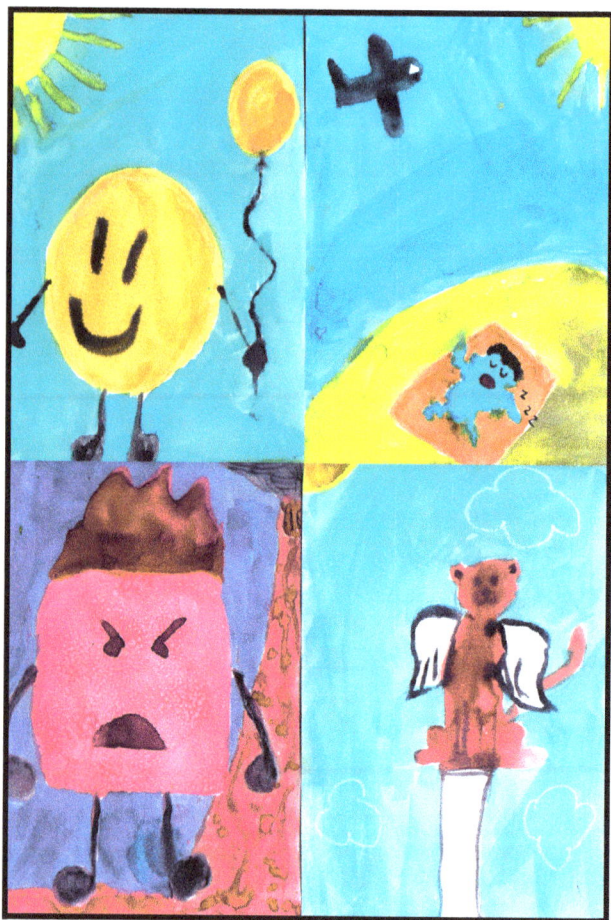

My Thoughts

In the depths of my heart
    are born many a thought.
Here they live and they die
    till new ones are wrought.

Some are full of sadness—
    oft they make me sigh.
They come when I am moody,
    but then they quickly die.

Some make me feel guilty;
    some make me feel mad.
Sometimes they're so lovely,
    the thoughts that I've had.

So I'll keep on thinking
    with a heart that's glad.
I'll welcome the good thoughts,
    and kick out the bad!

Dreams

I don't believe in dreams—
    not really.
They make me sad sometimes—
    that's silly.
Some dreams I wish could last—
    but that's wrong.
Some dreams are way too short—
    some too long.
At night I'm far away—
    I dream on.
But morning always comes—
    my dream's gone.

Spring

The winter snow is beautiful,
  I love the summer sun.
But most of all I love the trees
  that tell us Spring's begun.

I love their colorful splendor;
  it fills me with wonder and awe.
The beauty of the blossoms is
  of such you never saw.

Such peace can fill your soul
  in the magic time of Spring,
When God comes down
  with a loving hand—
    and touches everything.

I Have a Friend

I have a Friend who understands and cares
when other friends are too busy to help me.

I have a Guide who leads me to the Light
when darkness is all I can see.

I have a Teacher who teaches me of Love
and Truth and the key to the Heavenly gate.

I have a Comforter who promises perfect peace
in a world of worry, fear, and hate.

I have a Lover who loves me with a love
deeper than the ocean and stronger than the grave.

He is my Savior who shed His precious blood
to give me life eternal and my weary soul to save.

For Us

The robins are made to tell
  that spring is on its way.
The sunshine is made to give us
  life and hope for every day.

The stars are made to wish by
  and brighten the deepest night.
The moon is made to smile at us
  and aid us with guiding light.

The flowers are made to give us
  the hue and fragrance of joy.
The breeze is made to carry sweet scents
  and cool a warm summer day.

The trees are made to offer shade
  and a strong trunk to lean upon.
Music is made to soothe our hearts
  when a long, busy day is done.

God made all these things for us
  to fill our lives with cheer,
to make our days more pleasant
  and to make the Way more clear.

To Larry

They tell me it is puppy love
   and that it can't be true.
They say that I'm infatuated
   over the charms of you.
I don't care what they call it,
   because I know it's true,
For my heart is full of joy
   whenever I'm near you.

This feeling is so wonderful—
   it doesn't need a name.
I just know that since I've met you
   I've never been the same.
Since you've given me this feeling,
   my skies are never gray.
Whatever it is I only hope
   it never goes away.

He Loves Me

*(a song—accompanied
by my sister Beverly's
guitar playing)*

As I was walking down the road one day
my heart was heavy and my skies were gray.
A boy came along and made me glad again,
and I love him, I love him, I love him.

He took my hand and showed me the day;
birds started singing and clouds went away.
I saw the beauty of the earth anew,
when he said, "I love you, I love you."

Now we are singing as we walk along.
My heart's aglow and my life's a song.
He's shown me how happy life can be;
for he loves me, he loves me, he loves me!

Limerick

There was a young lady of Laos,
who screamed when she stepped on a mouse.
    She picked up a mop
    and gave it a whop!
That frightened young lady of Laos.

I Like To Eat!

(written tongue-in-cheek)

Oh, I love to eat!
It's my favorite pastime.
I eat in the morn,
and I eat at noontime.
I eat when the sun
comes over the prairie.
I eat and I eat
until I am weary.
An empty cupboard
is my greatest fear.
If I don't have food,
it brings many a tear.
People pity me,
but I sure don't see why.
I'm very happy—
All I need is a pie.
I'm getting so fat
that I'm going to burst.
But I can't help it
if I hunger and thirst.

Delight

As I walked down the valley
of endless delight,
I heard a fair melody
of bells tinkling bright.

Laughing and frolicking
were elves in a line
as they took turns sliding
down a ray of sunshine.

The fairies would dance
around in a ring,
then spin gold threads
and joyfully sing.

A rosy young maid
in gossamer gown
had silky hair that was
all flowing down.

The smiling flowers were
fluttering with mirth.
They drank in the sun,
and hugged the good earth.

I saw not a sign of
a frown on a face.
All was sunny and safe,
a beautiful place.

Solution For a Soul In Torment

*(inspired by a humorous story I read
while sick in bed.)*

'Twas the 17th of November,
  midst wind and rain,
when I noticed her look
  of anguish and pain.

Her face was contorted,
  her mouth all askew,
her anxious eyes saying,
  "What can I do?"

She wiggled and squirmed—
  couldn't sit still.
She swayed to and fro
  like a windmill.

She twiddled her thumbs;
  her eyes were crossed.
Then she twisted her legs,
  all composure lost.

She hopped on one foot
  and then the other.
Her soul was in torment;
  all hope smothered.

Then all of a sudden,
  her eyes took hope.
She dashed through a door
  like an antelope.

Then I saw the sign that
  ended the doom.
It had two simple words—
  "Ladies' Room."

Joy

(written for an English-class assignment)

To swing her swing as high as the sky,
    letting her hair blow free;
To chase a beautiful butterfly,
    or run along the sea;

To jump and skate and climb a tree—
    all movement free and wild;
To laugh and sing and dream a dream,
    this is the joy of a child.

To get an "A" in arithmetic,
    to buy a new school dress;
To be chosen "board moniter,"
    and play ball at recess;

To learn to spell and stories write,
    to race against the boys;
To find courage at day, no fear at night,
    this gives the school girl joy.

To go to parties with her friends,
    and in the choir sing;
To talk on the phone and messages send,
    and wear her boyfriend's ring;

To snuggle in a chair for hours
  and read a book at leisure;
To dream and pick some pretty flowers,
  is adolescent pleasure.

To look into her sweetheart's eyes
  and see a sparkle there;
To share her thoughts without disguise,
  and really, truly care;

To walk and talk with hand in hand,
  to give a little kiss;
To feel that someone understands—
  the lover's joy is this.

It's a Beautiful Day

The Robins sing,
  and the roosters crow.
The rising sun warms
  the valley below.

The sunlight dances
  on the warbling stream,
Sprinkling bright diamonds
  of red, blue and green.

The lively Linnet
  flicking through the trees
Sings soft and sweet
  duets with the breeze.

The sunlight is pouring
  down from above;
It's a beautiful day,
  and I'm in love!

About the Poet

Catherine (Cathy) Lawton has enjoyed producing written expression since she was a toddler scribbling in the margins of her preacher father's theology books. From age twelve to the present she has written and published poems, articles, stories, books, and blogs. In 1999 she started Cladach Publishing where, as publisher and editor, she enjoys giving other authors opportunities to share their creativity, expertise, and stories with readers.

Cathy can be found online at:

http://cladach.com/catherine-lawton/
Twitter: @Cath_Lawton
Author pages on Amazon.com and Goodreads
Selections of her recent poems are featured at:
http://www.altarwork.com/author/catherine-lawton/

She has been married to Larry for many years now. Highlights of their life together include sharing with others through music ministry, mission trips, and hospitality. They love to walk on the seashore and hike in the mountains. The Lawtons have two adult, married children and six grandchildren who give them great joy.

Two of their granddaughters, Isabelle Lawton and Breanna Slike, are the gifted young women whose artwork graces this volume.

.

www.ingramcontent.com/pod-product-compliance
Lightning Source LLC
Chambersburg PA
CBHW041923090426
42741CB00020B/3460